WESTMINSTER ABBEY

WEDNESDAY, APRIL 2ND, 1919

at 12 noon.

In Memory of the Officers, Warrant Officers, Non-Commissioned Officers and Men of the Household Cavalry who have died whilst serving with their Regiments or other formations during the War, 1914-1918.

" *Their glory shall not be blotted out and their name liveth to all generations.*"

—ECCLESIASTICUS *xliv., verses* 13 & 14.

"THERE is a healing magic in the night,
    The breeze blows cleaner than it did by day,
    Forgot the fever of the fuller light,
And sorrow sinks insensibly away
As if some saint a cool white hand did lay
Upon the brow, and calm the restless brain
The moon looks down with pale unpassioned ray—
Sufficient for the hour is its pain
Be still and feel the night that hides away heart's stain.
Be still and lose the sense of God in you.
Be still and send your soul into the all,
The vasty distance where the stars shine blue,
No longer antlike on the earth to crawl
Released from time and sense of great or small
Float on the pinions of the Night-Queen's wings ;
Soar till the swift, inevitable fall
Will drag you back into all the world's small things ;
Let for an hour be one with all escaped things "

(Found in the note-book belonging to a Subaltern Officer of the Household Cavalry when his kit came home, after he had been killed.)

2

INDEX.

PROGRAMME OF MUSIC.

Band of the 1st Regiment of Life Guards

G. J. MILLER, L.R.A.M., Bandmaster ;

Band of the 2nd Regiment of Life Guards

MAJOR C. W. H. HALL, M.V.O., Director of Music ;

AND THE

Band of the Royal Horse Guards **(***Blues***)**

MANUEL BILTON, Bandmaster ;

will play the following :

1. Eton Memorial March	*C. H. Lloyd*
2. " Angelus " from " Scenes Pittoresques "	*Massenet*
3. " When I am laid in Earth "	*Purcell*
4. " Thou art passing hence "	*Sullivan*
5. Suite from " Les Erinnyes "	*Massenet*

ORDER OF SERVICE.

When the King has taken his seat the following Hymn will be sung:

HYMN NO. 222 (A. & M.).

TEN thousand times ten thousand,
 In sparkling raiment bright,
 The armies of the ransom'd Saints
Throng up the steeps of light :
'Tis finish'd ! all is finish'd,
 Their fight with death and sin :
Fling open wide the golden gates,
 And let the victors in.

What rush of Alleluias
 Fills all the earth and sky !
What ringing of a thousand harps
 Bespeaks the triumph nigh !
O day, for which creation
 And all its tribes were made !
O joy, for all its former woes
 A thousand-fold repaid !

Oh, then what raptured greetings
 On Canaan's happy shore,
What knitting sever'd friendships up,
 Where partings are no more !
Then eyes with joy shall sparkle
 That brimm'd with tears of late ;
Orphans no longer fatherless,
 Nor widows desolate.

Bring near Thy great Salvation,
 Thou Lamb for sinners slain,
Fill up the roll of Thine elect,
 Then take Thy power and reign :
Appear, Desire of nations,
 Thine exiles long for home ;
Show in the heavens Thy promised sign :
 Thou Prince and Saviour, Come.   Amen.

Let us pray.

Lord, have mercy upon us.
Christ, have mercy upon us.
Lord, have mercy upon us

OUR Father which art in heaven, Hallowed be Thy Name, Thy kingdom come. Thy will be done, in earth as it is in heaven. Give us this day our daily bread ; And forgive us our trespasses, As we forgive them that trespass against us ; And lead us not into temptation, But deliver us from evil Amen.

O GOD, the Protector of all that trust in Thee, without Whom nothing is strong, nothing is holy ; Increase and multiply upon us Thy mercy ; that, Thou being our Ruler and Guide, we may so pass through things temporal, that we finally lose not the things eternal ; Grant this, O heavenly Father, for Jesus Christ's sake our Lord. Amen.

O ALMIGHTY God, Who hast knit together Thine elect in one communion and fellowship, in the mystical body of Thy Son Christ our Lord : Grant us grace so to follow Thy blessed Saints in all virtuous and godly living, that we may come to those unspeakable joys, which Thou hast prepared for them that unfeignedly love Thee ; through Jesus Christ our Lord. Amen.

PSALM XXIII 4.

YEA, though I walk through the valley of the shadow of death. I will fear no evil: for Thou art with me ; Thy rod and Thy staff comfort me

Sullivan

Then shall the Dean say as follows, all standing :

LET us now unite in reverent praise and thanksgiving for our brothers, the Officers, Warrant Officers, Non-Commissioned Officers and Men of the Household Cavalry, who in the Great War have laid down their lives for their King and their country

They were men who endured hardships with patience, and faced dangers with cheerfulness They fought right valiantly and well. They gave themselves , they gave their all, the promise of their manhood, the flower of their strength. Through them has been won the great victory ; through them we stand in the gateway of Peace , through them has been obtained the assurance of Freedom Theirs has been the great sacrifice ; and we thank God it has not been made in vain

From thanksgiving for their splendid offering we turn ourselves solemnized, yet, as we pray, inspired for the high responsibility of our simple daily duty ! May God so purify our desires and purge us from the selfishness of indolence and pride, that in our country's cause we may show ourselves not unworthy of our dear brothers departed, and with sure hope look forward to our joyful reunion with them hereafter in the higher service of our Risen Lord and Saviour

---

Silence shall be kept for a space

Then shall be sung by all standing ·

Praise God, from Whom all blessings flow,
Praise Him, all creatures here below,
Praise Him above, Angelic host,
Praise Father, Son, and Holy Ghost.   Amen.

7

Then shall the Dean say these prayers, all devoutly kneeling :

Let us pray

O ETERNAL Father, we draw nigh to Thee in this Church where our Kings and Queens are crowned, amid the memorials of Great Britain's most illustrious dead. We dedicate to Thy great glory the memory of our dead Brothers departed : Crown, we beseech Thee, with Thy loving mercy the offering of their brave lives : Grant unto them Thy eternal Peace, and unto all that mourn the blessing of Thy perfect comfort : We ask it in the Name of Him Who died and rose again for us all, Thy Son our Saviour Jesus Christ.   Amen.

O GOD of Spirits and of all flesh, Who hast trodden down death, hast subdued the devil, and hast given life to the world, do Thou, O Lord, give rest to the souls of these Thy servants, who have fallen asleep, in a place of light and verdure, in a place of refreshment, where sorrow, grief, and lamentation enter not.   Forgive them every sin of word, deed, or thought in Thy goodness and clemency , for there is no man who liveth and sinneth not : For Thou alone art without sin. Thy righteousness is an everlasting righteousness, and Thy word is truth ; For Thou art the Resurrection, the Life, and Refreshing of these Thy Servants who are fallen asleep.   O Christ our God, to Whom we ascribe glory with Thy Eternal Father, and Thy All-holy and Life-giving Spirit, now, always, and for ever and ever   Amen.

Then shall be sung by all standing :

HYMN No 391 (A & M.).

ONWARD, Christian soldiers,
    Marching as to war,
  With the Cross of Jesus
  Going on before
Christ the Royal Master
  Leads against the foe ,
Forward into battle,
  See, His banners go !
    Onward, Christian soldiers,
      Marching as to war,
    With the Cross of Jesus
    Going on before.

At the sign of triumph
  Satan's host doth flee ;
On then, Christian soldiers,
  On to victory.
Hell's foundations quiver
  At the shout of praise ,
Brothers, lift your voices,
  Loud your anthems raise.
                Onward, &c.

Like a mighty army
  Moves the Church of God ;
Brothers, we are treading
  Where the Saints have trod ;
We are not divided,
  All one body we,
One in hope and doctrine,
  One in charity.
                Onward, &c.

Crowns and thrones may perish,
  Kingdoms rise and wane,
But the Church of Jesus
  Constant will remain ,
Gates of hell can never
  'Gainst that Church prevail ;
We have Christ's own promise,
  And that cannot fail.
                Onward, &c.

Onward, then, ye people,
  Join our happy throng,
Blend with ours your voices
  In the triumph song ;
Glory, laud, and honour
  Unto Christ the King,
This through countless ages
  Men and Angels sing.
            Onward, &c.   Amen.

9   B

THE BLESSING

THE REGIMENTAL CALLS.

THE LAST POST

THE RÉVEILLÉ

GOD SAVE THE KING.

GOD save our gracious King,
Long live our noble King,
God save the King
Send him victorious,
Happy and glorious,
Long to reign over us,
God save our King.

Members of the Congregation are asked to stay in their places until the King has left the church

---

At the close of the service will be played :

THE REGIMENTAL MARCHES.

1st LIFE GUARDS.

Nominal Roll of Officers who have been killed in action, or who have died of wounds or disease during the European War, 1914-1918 :—

Abroad.

Major Lord John Cavendish, D.S.O.
Captain Lord Hugh Grosvenor.
Captain and Adjutant Sir R. V Sutton, Bart., M.C.
Lieutenant A L. E Smith, M.C.
Lieutenant H. A B. St. George.
Lieutenant Hon. G. Ward.
Lieutenant F. W Collins
Lieutenant G. T. Trafford.

At Home.

Lieutenant-Colonel E. B. Cook, M V O.
Captain the Hon. C. C Fellowes
Lieutenant Emmett, R.

Officers Attached.

1st LIFE GUARDS.

Abroad.

Captain E D F. Kelly
Lieutenant Hon W. R. Wyndham
Lieutenant J C. Close-Brooks.
Lieutenant Sir R. Levinge.
Lieutenant H Hulton Harrup.

Officers Attached Other Units.

Lieutenant O. S. Portal, Household Battalion.
Temporary 2nd-Lieutenant W. H. Wanklin.

1st LIFE GUARDS

Nominal Roll of Non-Commissioned Officers and Men who have been killed in action, or who have died of wounds or disease during the European War, 1914-1918 :—

Farrier-Staff-Corporal.

At Home.

2025 Farrier-Staff-Corporal Lambert, R. H

Abroad.

Corporals-of-Horse.

1972	Corporal-of-Horse	Bruce, P.
2326	,,	Coates, J.
2350	,,	Dawes, H. W.
2061	,,	Holmes, C. L.
2880	,.	Leggett, W. T.
2427	,,	McFeeley, G.
3088	,,	Storey, E. H.
2565	,,	Wise, J. W.

Corporals.

2693	Corporal	Adams, C.
2832	,,	Beal, A.
2802	,,	Castle, E. P.
2916	,,	Gibson, A. J.
2719	,,	Moore, F. W.
2549	,,	Neighbour, T. G.
2705	,,	Pate, T.
2569	,,	Rose, A.
2889	,.	Rowe, D. E.

Lance-Corporal.

3281 Lance-Corporal Kinnimouth, J.

Troopers.

3054	Trooper	Abrahams, M. G.
2714	,,	Arnold, A. J.
2770	,,	Black, J.
2429	,,	Bishop, W. A.
2780	,,	Berry, J.
2966	,,	Blackmore, A. J.
3461	,,	Brown, J. L.
3128	,,	Butler, F. J.
3360	,,	Bosworth, H.
2244	,,	Burton, V.
2273	,,	Breakspear, H.
2947	,,	Clay, W. H.
2920	,,	Dennes, V.
3593	,,	Downey, A.
3516	,,	Day, J. H.
3412	,,	Evans, T. L.
2828	,,	Ford, A. J.
2666	,,	Flaxman, W.
2025	,,	Fair, D. H.
2817	,,	Golding, C. G.
3171	,,	Green, E.
2922	,,	Helliwell, T. H
2900	,,	Hickling, H.
3111	,,	Hannan, T. S.
3388	,,	Hills, G.
3377	,,	Hunter, J.
4025	,,	Honey, J. H.
4224		Hammond, N. W.
2489	,,	Johnston, J.
2809	,,	Kimpton, E. C. G.
2965	,,	Lewry, E.
2411	,,	Levy, W. G
2827	,,	Lord, H
3596	,,	Lowe, C. H.
3103	,,	Moores, J. A.
3108	,,	Mawer, A.
3622	,,	Marks, R. W

3320	Trooper	McKillop, A.
3545	,,	McArthur, G
3359	,,	Newbrook, J
3056	,,	Nicholls, W. D.
2992	,,	Norris, C.
2818	,,	Pearce, C. H.
3080	,,	Pye, O. G.
3280	,,	Pattman, W.
3366	,,	Pell, H. W.
3482	,,	Penn, F. T. E.
2529	,,	Paget, F.
2759	,,	Proberts, J.
3429	,,	Palmer, S. C.
2929	,,	Roberts, W. H.
2859	,,	Russell, C. F.
2287	,,	Ruscoe A. C.
2882	,,	Redley, H.
3155	,,	Rimmer, C.
2682	,,	Rogers, F. S.
2870	,,	Scothern, J.
2686	,,	Sollars, S. E.
2345	,,	Streeter, H.
2447	,,	Savage, H.
2959	,,	Spoor, C. R.
2855	,,	Sillence, A. S.
3844	,,	Smith, A. C.
4169	,,	Spendlove, H. L
4280	,,	Simpkins, F. J
3518	,,	Toogood, G.
3003	,,	Thompson, W H.
2876	,,	Wood, J.
2979	,,	White, J. J
2739	,,	Woodward, W
2905	,,	Westley, R. W.
2741	,,	Whittaker, S.
2952	,,	Williamson, P.
3409	,,	Whitehead, W.
3044	,,	Winter, G.
4422	,,	West, R H
2852	,,	Westcott, P.

At Home.

3375	Trooper	Phillips, W C.
4664	,,	Woolfe, F B.

Nominal Roll of Non-Commissioned Officers and Men of the Cavalry of the Line, attached to 1st Life Guards, who have been killed in action or who have died of wounds or disease during the European War, 1914-1918 :—

Abroad.

Corporals-of-Horse.

20753	Corporal-of-Horse	Boyles, A., 1st Dragoons.
5358	,,	Colclough, H , 6th Dragoons.
5821	,,	Fraser, E., 3rd Dragoon Guards.
5852	,,	Middleton, W , 3rd Dragoon Guards.

Corporals.

6175	Corporal	Critchley, J., 1st (King's) Dragoon Guards.
5380	,,	Kirkpatrick, J , 1st (King's) Dragoon Guards.
6136	,,	Oliver, W , 1st Dragoon Guards.
21084	,,	O'Toole, C., 6th Dragoons.
288	,,	Turner, H , 1st (King's) Dragoon Guards.

Lance-Corporals.

5765	Lance-Corporal	Duff, C., 2nd Dragoons.
5193	,,	Maidment, E , 5th Dragoon Guards.
6318	,,	Rich, A. E., 1st (King's) Dragoon Guards.
5638	,,	Vann, W. H., 1st (King's) Dragoon Guards.

Privates.

5016	Private	Atwood, A., 2nd Dragoons
5684	,,	Anderson, E , 6th Dragoons
42	,,	Burnett, F M , 1st Dragoons
3583	,,	Brockwell, R , 1st Dragoon Guards.
4425	,,	Bow, W , 6th Dragoons.
1715	,,	Barwell, D., 3rd Dragoon Guards.
5321	,,	Bates, F , 6th Dragoon Guards.
6249	,,	Brown, T., 1st (King's) Dragoon Guards
5513	,,	Black, W , 6th Dragoons

15

8267	Private	Buffham, W A 2nd Dragoons.
6324	,,	Boddie, J H , 1st Dragoon Guards
653	,,	Bolton, W , 5th Dragoon Guards
5324	,,	Buckett, R , 5th Dragoon Guards
5836	,,	Cootes, H , 6th Dragoons
6196	,,	Cunningham, C H., 1st (King's) Drag Gds.
6300	,,	Cowley, G , 1st (King's) Dragoon Guards.
5409	,,	Campbell, E , 6th Dragoon Guards.
5507	,,	Dykes, W., 6th Dragoons
4946	,,	Davies, A , 6th Dragoons
5811	,,	Dormer, C., 6th Dragoons
5833	,,	Etchells, E., 6th Dragoons
5958	,,	Elliot, G , 1st Dragoon Guards
2520	,,	Green, C. C V., 6th Dragoons.
5211	,,	Gray, A J , 5th Dragoon Guards
2510	,,	Hamilton, J , 6th Dragoons
5223	,,	Hopkins, E. E , 5th Dragoon Guards.
8231	,,	King, T , 2nd Dragoons.
5726	,,	Keefe, W , 6th Dragoons.
6225	,,	Line, M , 1st (King's) Dragoon Guards.
8939	,,	Lewis, H , 6th Dragoon Guards
4507	,,	Moody, J , 6th Dragoons
4985	.,	Miller, W , 6th Dragoons
5342	,,	McDermott, H , 1st (King's) Dragoon Gds
6256	,,	Macdonald, T , 1st (King's) Dragoon Gds.
5421	,,	Naismith, T., 6th Dragoon Guards
5415	,,	Ordway, J , 3rd Dragoon Guards
6360	,,	Pickett, C , 6th Dragoons.
6031	,	Pike, J., 1st (King's) Dragoon Guards
2682	,,	Phillip, E. A , 6th Dragoon Guards.
5005	,,	Randall, J , 5th Dragoon Guards
4712	,,	Richards, F., 1st Dragoons
9180	,,	Rudge, E. J , 6th Dragoon Guards
5986	,,	Rowledge, E , 1st (King's) Dragoon Guards.
958	,,	Richardson, A , 1st Dragoons
6015	,,	Rose, F S , 1st (King's) Dragoon Guards
6886	,,	Spenceley, E. H , 7th Dragoon Guards.
5235	,,	Smart, R., 3rd Dragoon Guards
5381	,,	Skelly, S., 6th Dragoons
5963	,,	Simpson, E., 1st (King's) Dragoon Guards.
5308	,,	Taylor, A H , 1st (King's) Dragoon Guards
8458	,,	Wright, B , 3rd Dragoon Guards
4629	,,	Ward, T., 5th Dragoon Guards
5494	,,	Weston, P , 2nd Dragoon Guards
6675	,,	Woolward, E , 7th Dragoon Guards

Nominal Roll of 1st Life Guards, serving with Household Battalion, who have been killed in action, or who have died of wounds or disease during the European War, 1914-1918:—

Abroad

Squadron-Corporal-Major.

2899 Squadron-Corporal-Major Marriage, F. G.

Corporals-of-Horse.

3439 Corporal-of-Horse Dunn, G R.
4008　　　,,　　　　　Jeffery, J W.
4003　　　,,　　　　　Tilbury, J. W. P.

Corporals.

3990 Corporal Penfold, J. W.
4076　　,,　　Reid, W
3102　　,,　　Rudge, C T
3485　　,,　　Ruthven, J
3900　　,,　　Smedmore, V. D
3888　　,,　　West, F J

Lance-Corporals.

3744 Lance-Corporal Chandler, J
3940　　　　,,　　　　Warwick, J. C.

Troopers.

3945 Trooper Adams, E. V
3943　　,,　　Burch, A. P
4055　　,,　　Brown, A
4002　　,,　　Birkett, T E
3958　　,,　　Cooper, A R
4126　　,,　　Craig, T W
4157　　,,　　Chacksfield, E

3877	Trooper	Denny, W. T.
3875	,,	Dickinson, F.
3972	,,	Drew, A.
4124	,,	Daines, A.
4080	,	Darley, J. J.
4017	,,	Dawson, S.
4257	,,	Francis, J. E
3090	,,	Foster, F.
4106	,,	Gates, W. J.
3991	,,	Gill, J.
4140	,,	Gott, C. H.
3824	,,	Howell, R. W.
4033	,,	Holmes, A. E.
3951	,,	Hoyland, J.
3206	,,	Horne, J.
3433	,,	Hickson, L.
4031	,,	Jennings, G. A.
3934	,,	Jenkins, C. R.
3629	,,	Jeffery, R. C.
2759	,,	Morrison, F. G.
4172	,,	Morton, W. A.
3937	,,	Mewmarsh, P E.
3856	,,	Nye, H. R.
3763	,,	Parrott, A.
4039	,,	Pope, C. H.
3930	,,	Rawson, W.
4226	,,	Sermon, A. H.
4217	,,	Starkey, T. G.
4142	,,	Seep, F. H.
3925	,,	Scriven, G.
4047	,,	Thornton, A.
3882	,,	Travers, G
3639	,,	Twizell, T. H.
4024	,,	Tyler, A G.
3936	,,	Viney, H. W.
3874	,,	Wood, A.
4086	,,	Wheeler, O R.
3205	,,	White, R.
4211	,,	Watson, E
4082	,,	Wood, H. D.

At Home.

4159 Trooper Freeman, P. E V.

Nominal Roll of Men of the 1st Life Guards, serving with Household Siege Battery, who have been killed in action, or who have died of wounds or disease during the European War, 1914-1918 :—

Abroad.

Troopers.

200654	Trooper	Haimes, C. S.
200619	,,	Hirst, H.
200651	,,	Rogers, D.

2ND LIFE GUARDS.

— — —

Nominal Roll of Officers who have been killed in action, or who have died of wounds or disease during the European War, 1914-1918:—

Abroad.

Lieutenant-Colonel T. G J. Torrie
Major Hon H Dawnay.
Captain Hon A. O'Neill
Captain A M Vandeleur
Captain F. P. C Pemberton.
Lieutenant A G Murray Smith
Lieutenant Sir R G V Duff
Lieutenant A. C Hobson
Lieutenant C. E. Gunther
Lieutenant V. J Ferguson
2nd-Lieutenant W S Peterson
2nd-Lieutenant F D A. Blofeld.
2nd-Lieutenant S. J Townsend.
2nd-Lieutenant J A. Lovell
Temporary Lieutenant E W Butler
Temporary 2nd-Lieutenant L S. Ward Price.

Attached 2nd Life Guards.

Captain J F Todd, 30th C I H
Lieutenant J A S C. Anstruther, 6th Dragoon Guards
Lieutenant A. W Gale, 2nd Reserve Cavalry

2ND LIFE GUARDS.

Nominal Roll of Non-Commissioned Officers and Men who have been killed in action, or who have died of wounds or disease during the European War, 1914–1918 :—

Abroad.

Corporals-of-Horse.

2400	Corporal-of-Horse	Austin, A E
2206	,,	Backhouse, A H.
2216	,,	Dean, C. E
2405	,,	Ellison, A.
1921	,,	Marsh, R. J. F.
2420	,,	More, R. A.
2460	,,	Stevenson, W C.
2515	,,	Wells, C
2528	,,	Wilkins, A. H.

At Home.

2083	Corporal-of-Horse	Coxhead, C
2640	,,	Crane, G.
2705	,,	Mackie, P.
2468	Farrier-Staff-Corporal	Parker, A. D.

Abroad.

Corporals.

2961	Corporal	Bullivant, A.
2731	,,	Dean, A C N.
2671	,,	Forde, P.
2741	,,	Marchant, V.
2596	,,	Taylor, M G.

At Home.

3719 Corporal Michie, J.

Abroad.

Lance-Corporals.

2846	Lance-Corporal	Butler, W. H
2765	,,	Hartley, H. E
2763	,,	Langford, W. J.
2766	,,	Tremlett, A C.
3107	,,	Thomas, A. L

Troopers.

3731	Trooper	Aspland, E. A
3606	,,	Ayers, E A
2516	,,	Birdsall, W L
2633	,,	Bryce, J
2725	,,	Black, D
2789	,,	Bradshaw, F M
2810	,,	Boyce, H G.
3201	,,	Bourne, A.
2803	,,	Clements, T. H.
2871	,,	Clark, W.
2929	,,	Cooper, E.
2938	,,	Constable, J. T.
2695	,,	Davis, H.
2900	,,	De Laine, A E.
3300	,,	Dixon, H
3549	,,	Dutton, W. G.
3773	,,	Edghill, N. A.
2543	,,	Freeman, R.
3403	,,	Fawcett, B.
2535	,,	Goulding, C. R.
2668	,,	Herring, N. C.
2867	,,	Hagues, A G.
3480	,,	Hodgson, C.
3006	,,	Hawkins, G K.
2977	,,	Hutchinson, A. J.
2843	,,	Hawkins, W.
2919	,,	Johnson, B.
3207	,,	Jackson F.
2782	,,	Keene, F. C.
3351	,,	Kenny, J.
3171	,,	Kingshott, W.
2337	,,	Lindley, J. W.
2804	,,	Lovelock, W. J.
2630	,,	McKellar, F.

2778	Trooper	McCluskey, J.
2783	,,	Mills, F. E.
2894	,,	Monkhouse, J. W
3176	,,	Mendies, H
3241	,, ·	Maude, C. G.
2808	,,	Marriott G W
2451	,,	Owens, E H
2508	,,	Payne, F.
2634	,,	Potts, S J. A.
2756	,,	Potter, C J.
2812	.,	Pollard, A.
3155	,,	Puddifoot, J.
2898	,,	Randall, S. J.
2899	,,	Rouse, M. H.
2857	,,	Smith, R.
2905	,,	Stevens, S. J
2939	,,	Seymour, A. E.
2952	,,	Smout, A E
2674	,,	Tyler, H A
2712	,,	Taylor, C A
2970	,,	Towers, R.
2978	,,	Tilley, P. J.
3124	,,	Tyson, W.
2648	,,	Tully, G.
3941	,,	Tullett, H R.
2469	,,	Wackett, A.
2822	,,	Woods, A.
2877	,,	Wild, L.
3083	,,	Wright, F. S.
3181	,,	Witcomb, W.
3266	,,	Whatmough, G.
2823	,,	Wallis, C.

At Home.

2343	Trooper	Bailey, J. W.
2004	,,	Brown, W. T.
3933	,,	Bloom, G.
2060	,,	Freeman, H. S.
3650	,,	Hodges, H. W.
3249	,,	Morrison, J.
2328	,,	Phillips, A.
2999	,,	Robson, J.
3482	,,	Wilson, R.
2343	,,	Barley, J. W.

23

Nominal Roll of Non-Commissioned Officers and Men of the Cavalry of the Line, attached to the 2nd Life Guards, who have been killed in action, or who have died of wounds or disease during the European War, 1914-1918 :—

Abroad.

Corporal-of-Horse.

13324 Corporal-of-Horse Kelly, W., Lancers

Privates.

6360	Private	Archer, O J., 17th Lancers
6417	,,	Allison, C , 17th Lancers
6514	,,	Adams, 17th Lancers
1174	,,	Beck, —, 11th Hussars
4986	,,	Bugler, G , 11th Hussars
2484	,,	Batchelor, J , 3rd Dragoon Guards
4633	,,	Burgess, W G , 3rd Dragoon Guards
5098	,,	Bachelor, H , 3rd Dragoon Guards.
5292	,,	Buckley, E A , 3rd Dragoon Guards.
2498	,,	Bell, R , 6th Dragoons
4727	,,	Beckhurst, J. W., 6th Dragoons
6488	,,	Burke, J , 2nd Dragoon Guards
393	,,	Blackwell, E , 17th Lancers
5496	,,	Brandrum, W , 17th Lancers
6351	,,	Bryant, J. W , 17th Lancers
7458	,,	Brenchley, C F , 17th Lancers
2691	,,	Cameron, W , 6th Dragoons
481	,,	Chapman, G , 17th Lancers
4922	,,	Cox, J , 17th Lancers.
6487	,	Clark, J , 17th Lancers.
6520	,,	Cook, T , 17th Lancers.
328	,,	Crow, A , 16th Lancers.
4602	,,	Carver, E , 16th Lancers.
5315	,,	Dawes, T. R , 3rd Dragoon Guards.
4774	,,	Deverill, E., 17th Lancers.
6083	,,	Dockeray, R , 17th Lancers.
6551	,,	Davies, T., 17th Lancers.
6691	,,	Davison, J., 5th Lancers.

5211	Private	Darbyshire, H., 3rd Res. Cavalry Regt.
6404	,,	Ellis, H J , 21st Lancers
6421	,,	Ernscliffe, F. G , 11th Hussars.
1132	,,	Fisher, J , 6th Dragoon Guards.
1216	,,	Fuller, T , 6th Dragoon Guards.
6591	,,	Foreman, R., 5th Lancers.
5765	,,	Gilmartin, P., 3rd Dragoon Guards
4192	,,	Greiner, C W. H., 16th Lancers
4980	,,	Gore, W., 21st Lancers
5370	,,	Hancock, J , 3rd Dragoon Guards.
5497	,,	Hodgins, J , 6th Dragoons.
4373	,,	Hanna, C , 6th Dragoon Guards
5577	,,	Hewitt, A , 17th Lancers.
6197	,,	Hambley, B , 17th Lancers
6306	,,,	Hughes, B , 17th Lancers
10196	,,	Harrington, A , 3rd Res. Cavalry Regt.
4233	,,	Jacqueman, J., 3rd Dragoon Guards.
5500	,,	Jones, B J., 3rd Dragoon Guards.
4643	,,	Jones, A., 17th Lancers
4503	,,	Jordan, A. A , 16th Lancers
3839	,,	Kitchen, W , 17th Lancers.
5948	,,	Kingswell, A , 17th Lancers
477	,,	Lynch, O , 17th Lancers.
6149	,,	Lloyd, F C , 17th Lancers.
6481	,,	Lea, G E., 17th Lancers
7308	,,	Moore, J., 13th Hussars.
6962	,,	McAulay, W., 13th Hussars.
4314	,,	McLeod, R , 3rd Dragoon Guards.
3778	,,	Murray, A , 6th Dragoons
5391	,,	McDermott, P., 6th Dragoon Guards.
474	,,	Mason, G , 17th Lancers.
875	,	Mudd, S G , 17th Lancers
6346	,,	McLaren, D., 17th Lancers
3861	,,	Mead, J , 16th Lancers
5013	,,	Mews, W , 16th Lancers.
3356	,,	Moulson, C. E , 14th Hussars.
4718	,,	McIntosh, J , 13th Hussars
6454	,,	Neild, W , 17th Lancers.
1921	,,	Nevitte, A. H , 18th Hussars.
955	,,	O'Brien, P , 21st Lancers.
23722	,,	Oram, G , 18th Hussars.
4058	,,	Pacey, E , 3rd Dragoon Guards
6175	,,	Pettigrew, J A , 17th Lancers.

2nd LIFE GUARDS—Cavalry of Line Attached—*continued.*

6493 Private Pratt, J , 17th Lancers.
6523   ,,   Payne, H., 17th Lancers.
438   ,,   Pierson, A., 20th Hussars.
5394   ,,   Peacock, C., 3rd Reserve Cavalry Regt.
9884   ,,   Quirke, D., 2nd Dragoon Guards.
483   ,,   Quelch, C., 17th Lancers.
466   ,,   Rafferty, P., 17th Lancers.
6311   ,,   Robinson, F., 17th Lancers.
745   ,,   Squire, J , 3rd Dragoon Guards.
5210   ,,   Sullivan, P., 3rd Dragoon Guards.
5419   ,,   Stewart, W., 3rd Dragoon Guards.
6025   ,,   Strachan, D., 3rd Dragoon Guards.
8467   ,,   Sculler, A , 3rd Dragoon Guards.
6418   ,,   Shirtcliffe, J W., 2nd Dragoon Guards.
3837   ,,   Stephenson, F., 17th Lancers.
5520   ,,   Spencer, J. H., 17th Lancers.
6073   ,,   Saville, J , 17th Lancers.
9222   ,,   Sheehan, P , 11th Hussars.
4901   ,,   Thowtes, I. E., 3rd Dragoon Guards.
5732   ,,   Thrussell, A. G , 11th Hussars
6715   ,,   Watson, J., 8th Hussars
3653   ,,   White, H. J. F., 3rd Dragoon Guards.
3741   ,,   Wathen, A , 3rd Dragoon Guards.
4960   ,,   White, A. H., 3rd Dragoon Guards.
5106   ,,   Wickson, F. C., 3rd Dragoon Guards.
5384   ,,   Westbrook, W., 17th Lancers
6123   ,,   Wagstaffe, F., 17th Lancers
6204   ,,   Whitbread, F. S., 17th Lancers.
6356   ,,   Williams, J. W , 17th Lancers.
6473   ,,   Wassmer, H S., 17th Lancers.
4996   ,,   Wardle, A., 16th Lancers.
5226   ,,   Walker, J., 11th Hussars.

At Home.

3657 Private Fordham, R., 13th Hussars
1200   ,,   Lawson, —, 6th Dragoon Guards.
7934   ,,   Phillips, H , 2nd Dragoon Guards.
7668   ,,   Pearson, A., 3rd Reserve Cavalry Regt
5315   ,,   McCallum, A., 3rd Dragoon Guards.

Nominal Roll of 2nd Life Guards, serving with Household Battalion, who have been killed in action, or who have died of wounds or disease during the European War, 1914-1918 :—

Abroad.

Corporals.

3279	Corporal	Burrows, R. C.
3702	,,	Giles, F.
3817	,,	Jackson, A. E.
3339	,	Murrell, F J.
3568	,,	Sadler, W R.
3592	,,	Terrell, C. H.
3903	,,	Williams, E.

Lance-Corporals.

3700	Lance-Corporal	Hawthorne, E. F.
3801	,,	Oliphant, E. W.
3986	,,	Silver, A.
3687	,,	Weller, A. J.

Troopers.

3888	Trooper	Budd, H. V.
3346	,,	Cockshott, C.
3982	,,	Choules, A.
3287	,,	Carter, F.
3681	,,	Corcoran, J.
3913	,,	Collinson, J. G.
3661	,,	Danby, S
3827	,,	Dunne, A
3818	,,	Dodd, A. S.
3810	,,	Dunsdon, E. D.
3297	,,	Dickson, J. C.
3748	,,	Flowers, E W.
3704	,,	Grundy, G.
3684	,,	Griffiths, A. W.
3227	,,·	Hodgetts, W.
3688	,,	Higgins, F

3867	Trooper	Johnson, W. E.
3813	,,	King, H.
3703	,,	Leask, S.
3956	,,	Mallett, F. V.
3225	,,	Morris, F. R. W.
3831	,,	Newell, J. J.
3837	,,	Offer, E.
3196	,,	Part, F. G.
3588	,,	Pratt, P.
3984	,,	Parsons, H. W.
3854	,,	Read, E. J.
3156	,,	Sharp, A.
3966	,,	Sykes, R.
3526	,,	Shipton, J. R.
3834	,,	Townsend, F. C.
3969	,,	Waite, J. H.

Nominal Roll of 2nd Life Guards, serving with Household Siege Battery, who have been killed in action, or who have died of wounds or disease during the European War, 1914-1918 :—

Abroad.

Troopers.

4074	Trooper	Chapman, A G.
4188	,,	Lockhart, W J.
4097	,,	Scott, J. F.
3858	,,	Springford, I.
4113	,,	Williams, F. A.

ROYAL HORSE GUARDS.

Nominal Roll of Officers who have been killed in action, or who have died of wounds or disease during the European War, 1914-1918:—

Abroad.

Lieutenant-Colonels.

G. C. Wilson, M.V.O.
H. E. Brassey.

Majors.

H. W. Viscount Crichton, M.V.O., D.S.O.
L. A. Tilney, M.C.

Captains.

G. V. S Bowlby.
H. H. Wilson, D.S.O.
A. A. MacIntosh.

Lieutenants.

Lord C. S. Worsley.
Hon. C. E. A. Philipps.
P. V. Heath
G. V. Naylor-Leyland.
T. G. Davson
Baron de Gunsberg.

Second-Lieutenants.

Lord S. D. Compton.
W. L. Breese
Hon. A. Coke.
Hon. F. Lambton.
G. H. Pullen.
Viscount A. E. C. R. Wendover.
R. L. Sale.

At Home.

Brigadier-General.

Lord C. Binning, M.V.O.

Lieutenant-Colonel.

W. D. Mann-Thomson.

Majors.

Sir J C Willoughby, D S.O.
Hon. A H C Hanbury-Tracey, C.M.G.

Captain.

Viscount C. J. A. C. Ingestre.

Serving with other Units.

Abroad.

Captains.

A. L. Palmer, D.S O., Welsh Guards.
W. Newcombe, 1st Royal Dragoons.
C. H. Bodington, Household Battalion.

Lieutenants.

G. Stirling, M C , Scots Guards
S. Miller, Royal Inniskilling Fusiliers.
J. Jordon, 4th Dragoon Guards.
H. H. O. Bridgeman, Household Battalion.
R. H. L Whitelaw, Household Battalion.

ROYAL HORSE GUARDS.

Nominal Roll of Warrant Officers, Non-Commissioned Officers and Men who have been killed in action, or who have died of wounds or disease during the European War, 1914-1918 :—

Abroad.

Squadron-Quartermaster-Corporal.

776 Squadron-Quartermaster-Corporal Norris, F. H.

Corporals of Horse.

1481	Corporal-of-Horse	Cole, W.
1222	,,	Ervin, W G
1412	,,	Few, A G T.
1054	,,	Harris, J. C.
1462	,,	Harper, W. G. G.
1306	,,	Nelson, L. J.
1385	,,	Wells, W. A.

Corporals.

1305	Corporal	Baker, W.
1296	,,	Browning, M.
1688	,,	Claybyn, W A.
1341	,,	Eales, E W.
1609	,,	Owen, R
1533	,,	Waite, C. A
1454	,,	White, C H.

Lance-Corporals.

1475	Lance-Corporal	Burfield, F. H. T.
1564	,,	Dack, O. S.
2279	,,	Dickie, J. M , D.C.M.
1548	,,	Harper, F. H. A.

31

Saddle-Tree-Maker.

1756 Saddle-Tree-Maker Matthews, C. W.

Troopers.

2075	Trooper	Boyce, A F.
1717	,,	Brain, H
1491	,,	Cade, J. J.
2136	,,	Chase, F. W
1622	,,	Colsell, C E.
1769	,,	Cooper, S T.
1473	,,	Corlett, J.
1283	,,	Davies, J B.
1569	,,	Ditcher, F. C
1708	,,	Edgeley, C. S.
2148	,,	Forshaw, D.
1494	,,	Hastings, H A.
2322	,,	Hawes, E. J.
1884	,,	Hallett, T. B.
1601	,,	Hawkes, G. N. F.
1709	,,	Haynes, M G
1265	,,	Heron, A. E
2011	,,	Heywood, J
2122	,,	Holman, S F
2392	,,	Hoyland, G N.
1368	,,	Jenkins, F
1636	,,	King, C
1954	,,	Lancaster, T
2304	,,	Marshall, G
1252	,,	Meyer, G. E
1635	,,	Middleton, M
1559	,,	Molyneux, H B.
1597	,,	Morris, C. F
1456	,,	Munson, P E
2587	,,	Nicholson, E. J.
1417	,,	Oatley, S.
1482	,,	Ogglesby, H H
1840	,,	Pear, J W
1541	,,	Perry, W C
775	,,	Scott, R. W
1450	,,	Sherlock, D F.
2306	,,	Small, W E
1316	,,	Smith, G.
1415	,,	Terry, F.
1594	,,	Thurston, S. C.

Trumpeter.

1357 Trumpeter Scott, A H W G C

At Home

Squadron-Corporal-Major.

874 Squadron-Corporal-Major Shead, J. W. E.

Corporals-of-Horse.

1589 Corporal-of-Horse Munson, A. H.
1638   ,,   Heard, R. W. D.
1699   ,,   Dixon, R (Hon. Cpl.-Major).

Corporal.

2417 Corporal Farren, A.

Troopers.

2132 Trooper Avery, M J.
1428   ,,   Collyer, F H.
1900   ,,   George, H.
3110   ,,   Grant, A.
1991   ,,   Nelson, G. W.
1986   ,,   Newman, J. G. W.
1389   ,,   Viall, S. J.

Trumpeter.

1199 Trumpeter Fethon, C

Nominal Roll of Non-Commissioned Officers and Men of the Cavalry of the Line, attached to the Royal Horse Guards, who have been killed in action, or who have died of wounds or disease during the European War, 1914-1918:—

Abroad.

Corporals-of-Horse.

6659 Corporal-of-Horse Grainger, J., 8th Hussars.
45078   ,,   Piggott, 13th Hussars
5307   ,,   Rooke, E., 13th Hussars.

Corporal.

5268 Corporal Mutter, L. S , 20th Hussars

Lance-Corporals.

5464 Lance-Corporal Broom, W., 14th Hussars.
5256   ,,   Brown, J , 14th Hussars.
5645   ,,   Healey, A , 10th Hussars
5655   ,,   Owen, W. H , 14th Hussars.
10974   ,,   Riley, G , 11th Hussars
4143   ,,   Shaw, S., 14th Hussars

Privates.

9504 Private Arrigoni, A L , 20th Hussars.
5834   ,,   Anderson, A P , 13th Hussars.
10687   ,,   Arrowsmith, P., 20th Hussars.
4736   ,,   Austin, G W , 20th Hussars.
5764   ,,   Baker, S , 14th Hussars
5318   ,,   Barlow, T., 20th Hussars.
4499   ,,   Brooks, L J., 14th Hussars.
4582   ,,   Bunch, F J., 20th Hussars
8368   ,,   Cochrane, A , 6th Dragoon Guards.
4801   ,,   Cope, H A , 7th Hussars.
3075   ,,   Edwards, A. J , 14th Hussars.
4396   ,,   Foster, G , 20th Hussars.
1194   ,,   Gamage, W P , 13th Hussars.
45554   ,,   Gant, C., 7th Hussars.
4748   ,,   Garty, S., 20th Hussars
10686   ,,   Grainger, R., 20th Hussars
9954   ,,   Griffiths, C., 6th Dragoon Guards.
8390   ,,   Hadwen, G. S., 6th Dragoon Guards.
5055   ,,   Hall, J., 14th Hussars.
4649   ,,   Hallett, H., 20th Hussars.

6923	Private	Haines, H , 13th Hussars.
4872	,,	Hawksworth, W., 20th Hussars.
10678	,,	Hearne, W , 6th Dragoon Guards.
4531	,,	Higgleton, H , 20th Hussars.
4745	,,	Hillier, D , 13th Hussars
6865	,,	Hopkins, A , 8th Hussars.
8336	,,	Howie, G , 2nd Dragoons
16206	,,	Hutchison, A. Y., 11th Hussars.
3103	,,	Jones, E , 20th Hussars.
8441	,,	Kearney, A G , 6th Dragoon Guards.
5394	,,	Lathbury, J , 20th Hussars.
5319	,,	McColgan, C., 14th Hussars.
8772	,,	McCombe, J , 13th Hussars.
6542	,,	McSweeney, D , 8th Hussars.
9559	,,	McVay, T., 20th Hussars.
5083	,,	Montgomery, J , 6th Dragoon Guards.
4692	,,	Nicoll, A., 3rd Dragoon Guards.
4238	,,	Patterson, A., 14th Hussars
5587	,,	Pickavance, P , 14th Hussars.
7347	,,	Powell, B P , 3rd Dragoon Guards.
10439	,,	Read, L G , 20th Hussars.
6400	,,	Richardson, E., 8th Hussars.
4484	,,	Rothwell, A., 8th Hussars
9845	,,	Smith, F , 20th Hussars
5461	,,	Smith, C., 14th Hussars
6870	,,	Smith, E , 13th Hussars
4925	,,	Stevenson, J , 14th Hussars.
5472	,,	Strutt, H W , 20th Hussars
3070	,,	Sutton, W , 14th Hussars
5742	,,	Taunt, A F., 14th Hussars.
5408	,,	Taylor, J , 3rd Dragoon Guards.
6975	,,	Toombs, W , 13th Hussars.
5478	,,	Tucknott, W , 20th Hussars.
4034	,,	Tyrell, E , 14th Hussars.
5445	,,	Walker, J., 14th Hussars.
6138	,,	Weaver, H., 13th Hussars
5591	,,	Willcocks, G., 14th Hussars.
6473	,,	Wright, J., 8th Hussars.
4518	,,	Wright, L., 10th Hussars.

At Home.

6610	Private	Cronk, F., 8th Hussars.
5880	,,	Dean, J W., 7th Hussars
6352	,,	Gatland, W., 7th Hussars.
5546	,,	Guest, R , 14th Hussars.
5569	,,	Kemp, F., 13th Hussars.
5208	,,	Morris, G., 20th Hussars.

Nominal Roll of Royal Horse Guards, serving with Household Battalion, who have been killed in action, or who have died of wounds or disease during the European War, 1914-1918:—

Abroad.

Corporals-of-Horse.

2445	Corporal-of-Horse	Pateman, P. C
1719	,,	Rumney, F.
1805	,,	Reynolds, E. C
842	,,	Rayner, T. C H.
1051	,,	Sellars, E

Corporals.

771	Corporal	Farrar, J
2698	,,	Lee, H T
824	,,	Morris, L
348	,,	Ryan, S W. E
1691	,,	Scally, J W.

Lance-Corporals.

1156	Lance-Corporal	Boxall, R
778	,,	Gautrey, N. V
794	,,	Langtree, J E
473	,,	Mennell, W E
508	,,	Russell, V V
107	,,	Smith, W F

Troopers.

2624	Trooper	Abbott, W. H
1206	,,	Bardell, E
1108	,,	Burton, A. M
722	,,	Bruty, A J.
368	,,	Barnett, E
1660	,,	Ball, F. A
1742	,,	Campion, F. V
407	,,	Dolphin, F E

84	Trooper	Elliott, W R.
125	,,	Eyden, J. W
205	,,	Emmott, C
739	,,	Ecclestone, E
415	,,	Ford, G W
422	,,	Gapp, E J
39	,,	Holman, W
447	,,	Hilliam, W. P
782	,,	Hackett, F.
1216	,,	Haynes, J W
2705	,,	Jackson, F W
798	,,	Lewis, C. S
2708	,,	Munn, C. W.
141	,,	McElmurray, G.
187	,,	Morrison, J. F.
822	,,	Mann, J
825	,,	Meekings, H J.
826	,,	McNeill, R
1249	,,	Mullane, J
1186	,,	Nicholls, E.
2630	,,	Osborne, F W
1142	,,	Syddall, L
60	,,	Taylor, J W.
109	,,	Thompson, S
888	,,	Thompson, E R
891	,,	Underwood, J W
67	,,	Wale, A. G.
899	,,	Webb, C. G.
1248	,,	Walmsley, R G

Nominal Roll of Royal Horse Guards, serving with Household Siege Battery, who have been killed in action, or who have died of wounds or disease during the European War, 1914-1918:—

Abroad

197877 Paid Lance-Bombardier Smith, J. H.
197878 Gunner Andrews, A. H
197846   ,,   Goodey, A. G S
197835   ,,   Timms, R E.

HOUSEHOLD BATTALION.

*Nominal Roll of Officers, excluding those trans-
ferred from the Regiments of Household Cavalry,
who have been killed in action, or who have died
of wounds or disease during the European War,
1914-1918 :—*

Lieutenant C S Beechcroft.
2nd-Lieutenant K W Bird.
Temporary 2nd-Lieutenant N Bonham-Carter
Temporary 2nd-Lieutenant W. H Bolitho
Temporary 2nd-Lieutenant T G Bower
Lieutenant A P. Godfrey
Temporary 2nd-Lieutenant J. E Lowrie.
Temporary Captain H C Pember
Temporary 2nd-Lieutenant C V Rice
Lieutenant L Scott
Temporary 2nd-Lieutenant L F Stockwood
Temporary 2nd-Lieutenant J D'u Tyrwhitt-Drake.
2nd-Lieutenant O Wakefield
Temporary 2nd-Lieutenant S D Williams
Temporary 2nd-Lieutenant G. E. Whitelaw

HOUSEHOLD BATTALION.

Nominal Roll of Warrant Officers, Non-Commissioned Officers and Men who were transferred to the Household Battalion from Regiments other than the Household Cavalry, who have been killed in action, or who have died of wounds or disease during the European War, 1914-1918:—

R.-Q.-M.-C.-M.

1981 R.-Q.-M.-C.-M. Jones, J H , Staffordshire Yeomanry.

Corporal-of-Horse.

1957 Corporal-of-Horse Twyman, G. W., East Kent Yeomanry·

Acting-Corporal-of-Horse.

1963 Acting-Corporal-of-Horse Nicholls, T.W , Norfolk Yeomanry.

Privates.

1707	Private	Anderson, H T , East Kent Yeomanry
1716	,,	McCartney, G., East Kent Yeomanry
1718	,,	Pattason, A. D East Kent Yeomanry.
1731	,,	Yates, A E , East Kent Yeomanry
1737	,,	Carrier, H. T , East Kent Yeomanry
1739	,,	Kenneday, C J , East Kent Yeomanry.
1749	,,	Kay, R , East Kent Yeomanry.
1757	,,	Bowdery, C H , East Kent Yeomanry.
1761	,,	Butchers, G F , Sussex Yeomanry.
1767	,,	Squibb, H. A , Sussex Yeomanry.
1768	,,	Griffiths, S., Sussex Yeomanry.
1774	,,	Beall, G P., Sussex Yeomanry.

1777	Private	Holloway, P W., Sussex Yeomanry
1778	,,	Smith, H G , Sussex Yeomanry
1780	,,	Whiteman, E M , Sussex Yeomanry
1785	,,	Simmonds, H C , Sussex Yeomanry
1806	,,	Woodhouse, H L , West Kent Yeomanry.
1814	,,	Newell, A E , West Kent Yeomanry.
1821	,,	Bent, F E , West Kent Yeomanry.
1823	,,	Berryman, C. H., West Kent Yeomanry.
1829	,,	Pirie, W , Lanark Yeomanry
1836	,,	McSharry, F , Lanark Yeomanry
1839	,,	Thomson, T , Lanark Yeomanry
1840	,,	Hannah, S , Lanark Yeomanry
1844	,,	McMurdo, I , Lanark Yeomanry
1850	,,	Hawthorne, J , Lanark Yeomanry
1851	,,	Clark, G F , Lanark Yeomanry
1852	,,	Marshall, W. G , Lanark Yeomanry
1860	,,	O'Neill, P , Lanark Yeomanry
1867	,,	Turnbull, J , Lanark Yeomanry
1870	,,	Bertram, G., Lanark Yeomanry
1884	,,	Blunt, S. J , Norfolk Yeomanry
1891	,,	Carver, H J , Norfolk Yeomanry.
1896	,,	Groves, H , Norfolk Yeomanry
1902	,,	Nightingale, W., Norfolk Yeomanry
1909	,,	Sargeant, E T , Norfolk Yeomanry
1910	,,	Scott, T. J , Norfolk Yeomanry
1967	,,	Pryke, G S., Norfolk Yeomanry.
1972	,,	Thurlow, A E , Norfolk Yeomanry
1919	,,	Watson, R , Ayr Yeomanry
1922	,,	Jones, J., Ayr Yeomanry
1924	,,	Cairns, J , Ayr Yeomanry.
1932	,,	McInnes, J , Ayr Yeomanry
1933	,,	Dowie, W , Ayr Yeomanry
1943	,,	Paton, W G , Ayr Yeomanry

Nominal Roll of Non-Commissioned Officers and Men who did not belong to the three Household Cavalry Regiments, but joined the Household Brigade direct, who were killed in action, or who have died of wounds or disease during the European War, 1914-1918.

Lance-Corporals.

1558	Lance-Corporal	Hogg, J.
1593	,,	Strutt, R. H.
1702	,,	Spillman, F. C.

Troopers.

460	Trooper	Langford, S. L.
817	,,	Leech, R.
1404	,,	Stock, W. F.
1409	,,	Butterfield, A. J.
1412	,,	Gill, H.
1420	,,	Burnett, C. L.
1423	,,	Mitchell, W.
1429	,,	Thistlethwaite, E.
1430	.,	Rawson, R. F.
1439	,,	Forkes, A. B.
1440	,,	Salter, W G N.
1441	,,	Parsons, W J.
1446	,,	Wintle, F.
1448	,,	Musselle, F.
1450	,,	Fry, P.
1458	,,	Belchamber, W.
1462	,,	Dewey, F.
1466	,,	Carter, F. R.
1471	,.	Clinker, J.
1476	,,	Green, F.
1481	,,	Ronalds, S.
1483	,,	Slinger, H.
1491	,,	Kenkins, J. S.
1494	,,	Merriman, D
1509	,,	Hawks, W. J.
1519	,,	Hargreaves, H.
1526	,,	Jones, E. R.
1527	,,	Mawson, C. H.
1545	,,	McLachlan, G.

1548	Trooper	Weeding, G.
1552	,,	Morrice, J.
1563	,,	Wilson, J. J.
1567	,,	Pitt, E.
1569	,,	Pollitt, S.
1572	,,	Thompson, W.
1575	,,	Button, W H.
1584	,,	Strong, W. N.
1610	,,	Preston, J A.
1613	,,	Heyes, P. H.
1614	,,	Sharples, J. C.
1616	,,	Barnaby, C E.
1620	,,	Berry, W. J
1636	,,	Bennett, E.
1637	,,	Le Feaver, C.
1639	,.	Hatfield, C. E.
1644	,,	Aspin, W
1645	,,	Lewis, W. J.
1649	,.	Harmer, W.
1650	,,	Chatfield, G. H.
1651	,,	Quarnton, T. A.
1660	,,	Tansell, B.
1673	,,	Tindale, —.
1678	,,	Neeves, J. W.
1679	,,	Clarke, E.
1680	,,	Ratley, L
1682	,,	Meeson, T
1688	,,	Firth, J. N.
1690	,,	Howell, F. P.
1700	,,	Wilkinson, T. W.
1701	,,	Boyce, J. F.
1704	,,	Thirkettle, G.
1708	,,	Anderson, A.
1717	,,	McLachlan, J B.
1726	,,	Gambrill, W.
1879	,,	Ralph, J.
1907	,	Rudram, F V.
1929	,,	McLean, J
1936	,,	Mitchell, E. D.
1940	,,	Dewar, R. J. M.
2028	,,	Hobbs, J. T.
2033	,,	Vines, W.
2044	,,	Sykes, T. E.
2045	,,	Carter, F.
2046	,,	Kensett, W. B.

2047	Trooper	Ibbotson, G. T
2048	,,	Dow, J.
2052	,,	Wilhams, W. J
2067	,,	Webb, L. R.
2068	,,	Jeffery, G. C
2077	,,	Cooper, S A.
2080	,,	Robinson, R
2089	,	Lawton, L.
2093	,,	Herriett, C. R
2095	,,	Tattle, H. R.
2104	,,	Wroot, G. E
2115	,,	White, A.
2122	,,	Compton, W. G
2123	,,	Whitehead, E. G.
2128	,,	Dow, E. J.
2136	,,	Miller, T L.
2138	,,	Boxall, E. B
2141	,	Bray, R.
2142	,,	Dann, A E
2143	,,	Barton, J. E
2145	,,	Sargeant, F. W. B.
2147	,,	Hancock, C
2151	,,	Barnes, G. E.
2154	,,	Potts, H. R
2156	,,	Mellor, F
2158	,,	Kingsnorth, A N.
2161	,,	Jennings, W. A.
2163	,,	Austin, F.
2167	,,	Arnsworth, W.
2173	,,	Tucker, E. C.
2175	,,	Yarwood, J. B.
2185	,,	Knott, F J
2199	,,	Lee, T.
2200	,,	Nolan, W. J.
2207	,,	Randal, S.
2228	,	Mumby, W H.
2231	,,	Dawney, F.
2233	,,	Hargraves, I. ·
2243	,,	Haworth, F.
2254	,,	Barker, E
2264	,,	Pratt, A. G D.
2272	,,	Heath, F J.
2279	,,	Windle, K.
2280	,,	Barter, J.
2282	,,	Lovell, G R.

2288	Trooper	Smith, G. R.
2289	,,	Taylor, H. E.
2310	,,	Stamforth, W
2311	,,	Lees, A.
2315	,,	Butterworth, H.
2317	,,	Small, A H.
2319	,,	Ingleby, B.
2328	,,	Lucas, B.
2334	,,	Riddock, J.
2354	,,	Stephens, J.
2359	.	Morrison. A. A
2362	,,	Gardener, E
2368	,,	Hoath, A. S.
2374	,,	Sanders, C. J.
2379	,,	Surrell, W. J
2392	,,	Potter, J. S
2394	,,	Wedge, C
2402	,,	Barnes, R E
2408	,	Hope, H. E
2418	,,	Harrison, W J
2420	,,	Rose, S.
2422	,,	Phillips, C
2423	,,	Lee, S S
2427	,,	Baxter, W W.
2431	,,	Sadler, W
2437	,,	Kennett, E. C.
2454	,,	Kimber, F.
2457	,,	Howard, W. N.
2467	,,	Cass, J.
2470	,,	Langhorne, S
2479	,,	Monks, C.
2490	,,	Birch, H.
2495	,,	Head, A. B
2497	,,	Howard, G.
2501	,,	Helmer, E. W.
2502	,,	Jenner, S.
2511	,,	Bennett, H.
2515	,,	Jones, D.
2523	,,	Thomas, H. W.
2536	,,	Harrison, F E.
2540	,,	Allsop, S
2546	,,	Holyrake, R C
2554	,,	Kilgner, J. M.
2555	,,	Hill, A. B
2575	,,	Blackburn, R. W.

2578	Trooper	Faithfull, A. W.
2583	,,	Baldwin, J.
2585	,,	Haskell, W. J
2595	,,	Soper, E B.
2599	,,	Hider, C. T
2607	,,	Eustone, S
2608	,,	Hogan, W.
2612	,,	Barnes, J. K.
2616	,,	Grellier, F
2617	,,	Porter, N.
2620	,,	Riches, C. E
2623	,,	Turner, W R
2624	,,	Stratton, F. W
2636	,,	Pickworth, W A
2639	,,	Robb, J.
2651	,,	Ashfield, A J
2654	,,	Parsons, W
2655	,,	Butt, W. F.
2679	,,	Mitchell, E. N.
2690	,,	Hurd, J L.
2708	,,	Mann, C W.
2722	,,	Tattersall, E.
2729	,,	McCartney, J
2734	,,	Ward, W.
2748	,,	Page, W. J.
2778	,,	Seddon, A. H.
2781	,,	Brown, S.
2784	,,	Darbyshire, T
2795	,,	Rathbone, F
2804	,,	Ford, F C
2867	,,	Crawford, W.
2990	,,	Bennett, E
3013	,,	Appleby, S.
3032	,.	Errington, G
3048	,,	Thompson, A
3071	,,	Fullerton, C. E. G.
3090	,,	Lewis, W. J
3102	,,	Pearson, J.
3124	,,	Thompson, F. L.
3166	,,	Maple, A H J
3170	,,	Redman, J. W.
3244	,,	Kiddie, M.
3278	,,	Harris, W. N.
3313	,,	Tabern, S.
3314	,,	Taylor, J. W.
3328	,,	Evans, G. L.

45

GUARDS MACHINE GUN REGIMENT.

Nominal Roll of Warant Officers, Non-Commissioned Officers and Men of the Household Cavalry who were killed in action or who died of wounds or disease while serving with the Guards Machine Gun Regiment during the European War, 1914-1918:—

Warrant Officers Class II.

2048 Squadron-Corporal-Major Attenborough, G., D C.M., 1st Life Guards

3372   ,,   Brown, W. W , 1st Life Guards

3000   ,,   Webb, W , 1st Life Guards.

Squadron-Quartermaster-Corporals.

2315 Squadron-Quartermaster-Corporal Horsman, A., M M , 1st Life Guards

2027   ,,   ,,   Vessey, G., 1st Life Guards

Corporals-of-Horse.

2673 Corporal-of-Horse Boylin, G , 1st Life Guards.

2798   ,,   Fleming, J., D C.M., 1st Life Guards

2960   ,,   Waspe, W., 1st Life Guards.

Acting-Corporal-of-Horse.

4339 Acting-Corporal-of-Horse Blommer, G., 2nd Life Guards.

Corporal.

3995 Corporal Riddler, W., 1st Life Guards.

Acting Corporals.

4434 Acting-Corporal Dash, E. E., 2nd Life Guards.
4911   ,,   Webling, B , 2nd Life Guards

Lance-Corporals.

3647 Lance-Corporal Finlay, W , 1st Life Guards.
3004   ,,   Finnimore, H , 1st Life Guards
3112   ,,   Goddard, D , 1st Life Guards
5525   ,,   Greaves, A. K., Royal Horse
                  Guards.
3721   ,,   Penn, F , 1st Life Guards

Trumpeter.

2556 Trumpeter Godwin, C , 1st Life Guards.

Troopers.

3192 Trooper Ainslie, J., 1st Life Guards
3341   ,,   Berterelli, J , 1st Life Guards
3640   ,,   Clay, E , 1st Life Guards
3370   ,,   Derenzy, T , 1st Life Guards
3396   ,,   Douglas, R , 1st Life Guards
3168   ,,   Downing, A , 1st Life Guards
3328   ,,   Fenwick, R , 1st Life Guards
3917   ,,   Geeson, H , 1st Life Guards
3548   ,,   Gray, J , 1st Life Guards.
3104   ,,   Green, L., 1st Life Guards
3216   ,,   Hamilton, A , 1st Life Guards.
3120   ,,   Harwood, H , 1st Life Guards.
3371   ,,   Hobday, W., 1st Life Guards.
2883   ,,   Hopper, T , 1st Life Guards.
3947   ,,   Isherwood, F., 1st Life Guards.
3600   ,,   Juniper, A , 1st Life Guards
3860   ,,   Keeble, H , 1st Life Guards.
3149   ,,   Kercher, S T , 1st Life Guards.
3725   ,,   King, C , 1st Life Guards
3503   ,,   Lawrence, B , 1st Life Guards.
3634   ,,   Lindridge, A G , 1st Life Guards.
3038   ,,   Mariner, E., 1st Life Guards
3029   ,,   Moody, G , 1st Life Guards.
3698   ,,   Needs, E. L., 1st Life Guards.

47   D 2

3278 Trooper Ogbourne, H., 1st Life Guards.
3064 ,, Page, H., 1st Life Guards.
3430 ,, Ray, F , 1st Life Guards
3091 ,, Robb, A., 1st Life Guards.
3149 ,, Rowland, A , 1st Life Guards.
3609 ,, Royce, E , 1st Life Guards.
3127 ,, Sartin, A , 1st Life Guards.
3080 ,, Staniforth, H , 1st Life Guards.
3033 ,, Taylor, H , 1st Life Guards.
3050 ,, Thomas, F , 1st Life Guards.
3090 ,, Toberty, H , 1st Life Guards.
3681 ,, Turner, H., 1st Life Guards.
3035 ,, Vye, G., 1st Life Guards.
3779 ,, Worne, L , 1st Life Guards
3237 ,, Wright, B., 1st Life Guards.
3029 ,, Young, O , 1st Life Guards.

Musician.

3086 Musician Smith, S., 1st Life Guards.

Troopers.

4317 Trooper Barber, C. W., 2nd Life Guards.
4368 ,, Buchanan, J , 2nd Life Guards.
4162 ,, Edis, R , 2nd Life Guards.
4475 ,, Fairchild, G B., 2nd Life Guards.
4224 ,, Hammond, N., 2nd Life Guards.
4025 ,, Honey, J , 2nd Life Guards
4074 ,, Ireland, T., 2nd Life Guards.
4022 ,, Keen, F., 2nd Life Guards.
4062 ,, Maskell, J. H., 2nd Life Guards.
4190 ,, Merrick, F. R , 2nd Life Guards.
4703 ,, Nesham, H. J., 2nd Life Guards.
4737 ,, Pickhard, F. H., 2nd Life Guards.
4787 ,, Savage, C , 2nd Life Guards.
4280 ,, Simpkins, F , 2nd Life Guards
4151 ,, Smith, R. F , 2nd Life Guards.
4092 ,, Smith, C. J., 2nd Life Guards.
4169 ,, Spendlove, H., 2nd Life Guards.
4176 ,, Stallwood, A , 2nd Life Guards.
4836 ,, Steeds, F., 2nd Life Guards.
4844 ,, Stone, T. P., 2nd Life Guards.
4422 ,, West, R., 2nd Life Guards.
5074 ,, Collins, R., Royal Horse Guards.

Printed by GALE AND POLDEN, LTD., *London and Aldershot.*

* 9 7 8 1 8 4 3 4 2 6 4 8 6 *